T0276259

RECONSTRUCTION
AND ITS AFTERMATH
Freed Slaves after the Civil War

RECONSTRUCTION
AND ITS AFTERMATH
FREED SLAVES AFTER THE CIVIL WAR

MICHELLE DAKOTA BECK

MASON CREST
PHILADELPHIA | MIAMI

MASON CREST
450 Parkway Drive, Suite D, Broomall, Pennsylvania 19008
(866) MCP-BOOK (toll-free) • www.masoncrest.com

© 2020 by Mason Crest, an imprint of National Highlights, Inc.

Printed and bound in the United States of America.

CPSIA Compliance Information: Batch #RGSL2019.
For further information, contact Mason Crest at 1-866-MCP-Book.

First printing
1 3 5 7 9 8 6 4 2

ISBN (hardback) 978-1-4222-4405-0
ISBN (series) 978-1-4222-4402-9
ISBN (ebook) 978-1-4222-7420-0

Library of Congress Cataloging-in-Publication Data
on file at the Library of Congress

Interior and cover design: Torque Advertising + Design
Production: Michelle Luke

Publisher's Note: Websites listed in this book were active at the time of publication. The publisher is not responsible for websites that have changed their address or discontinued operation since the date of publication. The publisher reviews and updates the websites each time the book is reprinted.

QR CODES AND LINKS TO THIRD-PARTY CONTENT

TABLE OF CONTENTS

KEY ICONS TO LOOK FOR:

Words to Understand: These words with their easy-to-understand definitions will increase the reader's understanding of the text while building vocabulary skills.

Sidebars: This boxed material within the main text allows readers to build knowledge, gain insights, explore possibilities, and broaden their perspectives by weaving together additional information to provide realistic and holistic perspectives.

Educational videos: Readers can view videos by scanning our QR codes, providing them with additional educational content to supplement the text. Examples include news coverage, moments in history, speeches, iconic sports moments, and much more!

Text-Dependent Questions: These questions send the reader back to the text for more careful attention to the evidence presented there.

Research Projects: Readers are pointed toward areas of further inquiry connected to each chapter. Suggestions are provided for projects that encourage deeper research and analysis.

Series Glossary of Key Terms: This back-of-the-book glossary contains terminology used throughout this series. Words found here increase the reader's ability to read and comprehend higher-level books and articles in this field.

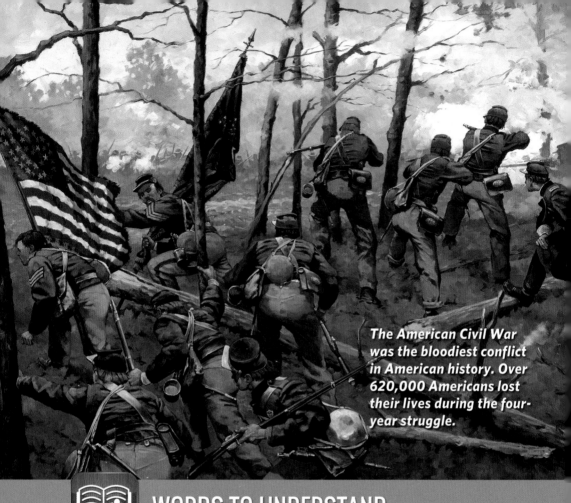

The American Civil War was the bloodiest conflict in American history. Over 620,000 Americans lost their lives during the four-year struggle.

 # WORDS TO UNDERSTAND

During the Civil War, the **border states** were slaveholding states that remained loyal to the Union. They included Delaware, Maryland, Kentucky, Missouri, and, eventually, West Virginia.

The **Fire Eaters** were leaders of the Democratic Party who were from slaveholding states. In the late 1850s they began to encourage southern states to form a new nation in order to protect the slave system in those states.

A **garrison** is a fortified military post. The word can also be used to describes the troops that defend a fort.

Popular sovereignty is a political doctrine asserting that the government is created by and subject to the will of the people.

CHAPTER 1

A Broken Nation

Disagreements between the northern and southern sections of the country had been building since the early nineteenth century. There were important economic and social differences between the North and the South. Tensions rose throughout the 1850s, as the nation wrestled with the issue of slavery, and reached a boiling point after the election of Abraham Lincoln as president in November 1860.

Lincoln was the candidate of the Republican Party, which had been formed just a few years earlier. Most Republicans believed the system of chattel slavery in the South was evil and wanted to see it eliminated. However, slavery was permitted under the US Constitution, so during his election campaign Lincoln had promised not to interfere with slavery in the states where it already existed. He said he would continue to enforce the laws that protected slavery, such as the Fugitive Slave Act, which required northerners to help return escaped slaves to their masters.

More Americans In 1860 were members of the Democratic Party than the Republican Party. Yet the Democrats were divided on the issue of slavery. Northern Democrats supported Stephen A. Douglass, a senator from Illinois. Douglass wanted to allow the people who settled in western territories to decide for themselves if they wanted to permit slavery or not—a doctrine that became known as **popular sovereignty**. Southern Democrats backed John

After Abraham Lincoln was elected president in 1860, eleven southern states tried to break away from the United States. Lincoln's commitment to restore the Union using whatever means he could, including an end to slavery, changed the United States forever.

C. Breckinridge, the sitting vice president, who promised to extend slavery into all new western territories.

The split enabled Lincoln to win the 1860 election, carrying most of the electoral votes from the Northern states. Despite Lincoln's pre-election statements, some prominent southern leaders, nicknamed the **Fire Eaters**, argued that the Republican election victory would mark the end of slavery and would disrupt the established way of life in the South. Several of the slaveholding states soon declared their intent to break away from the United States and form a new country.

On December 20, 1860, the people of South Carolina voted in a state convention to secede from the United States. The next month, Mississippi, Florida, Alabama, Georgia, Louisiana, and Texas also voted to secede. By the time Lincoln was sworn in as president on March 4, 1861, the rebellious states had agreed to work together as the Confederate States of America. They formed a government, and elected Jefferson Davis as their president.

In April, Confederates attacked and captured the federal **garrison** at Fort Sumter, in the harbor of Charleston, South Carolina. They seized weapons there for the Confederacy. In response, President Lincoln issued a called for troops to put down the rebellion. Most of the northern states answered the call by drafting soldiers, but four additional southern states—Virginia, Tennessee, North Carolina, and Arkansas—joined the Confederacy. The American Civil War was underway.

JUSTIFICATIONS FOR THE WAR

The Fire Eaters and other Confederate leaders claimed that their states had the right to leave the United States at any time. Once they seceded, the states withdrew their representatives from the US Congress and declared their allegiance to the new Confederate government. They no longer considered themselves bound by

A white overseer on horseback observes black workers picking cotton. By 1860, there were approximately 4 million black slaves in the southern states. Concerns that the slave system might be abolished led southern leaders to attempt to secede from the Union.

This map shows the United States in 1861. Several border states where slavery was legal remained loyal to the Union, as did the mountainous western part of Virginia. West Virginia would be admitted as a separate state in 1863.

US laws. From the southerners perspective, the Civil War was a conflict between two separate countries: the United States and the Confederate States.

President Lincoln and other northern leaders disagreed with this perspective. Under the US Constitution, states did not have the authority to withdraw from the United States. This meant the Civil War was an unlawful rebellion by the southern states against federal authority. The US government had the right to use force against the rebels to ensure that federal laws were respected and obeyed throughout the southern states.

Lincoln insisted publicly that the purpose of fighting the Civil War was to preserve the union of the thirty-four states that were part of the United States in 1861. It was not, Lincoln stressed, about giving freedom to slaves or ensuring the rights of black Americans. Lincoln had political reasons for taking this approach. In 1861 most white northerners would not support a war to free black people, but they would fight to preserve their country. Lincoln also hoped this approach would keep slave-holding states like Delaware, Kentucky, Maryland, and Missouri from joining the Confederacy. These **border states** never voted to secede from the United States, and the slave system continued to be legal there.

Not everyone agreed with Lincoln's approach, however. Once the war broke out, abolitionists in the North argued that the federal government's goals should include freeing the slaves and punishing rebellious slaveholders. Members of the Republican Party who supported the abolitionist position were known as Radical Republicans. They included Congressmen like Senator Charles Sumner of Massachusetts, Senator Benjamin Wade of Ohio, and Representative Thaddeus Stevens of Pennsylvania. The Radical Republicans pointed to the numerous compromises and agreements over slavery that the northern and southern states had made during the preceding decades. They argued that for a permanent peace between North and South to be possible, slavery in the United States had to end.

Scan here to learn more about the abolitionist movement.

General John C. Frémont was a respected explorer and soldier who had been the Republican Party's candidate for president in 1856. As commander of Union forces west of the Mississippi River, Frémont issued a proclamation in August 1861 banning slavery in Missouri. Lincoln feared this might drive the border states out of the Union, so he rescinded the order and removed Frémont from his post.

"The rebels are numerous and powerful, and their cause is Slavery," Sumner said in an October 1861 speech. "In the name of Slavery, and nothing else, has all this crime, destruction, and ravage been perpetrated; and the work is still proceeding.... It is often said that the war will make an end of Slavery. This is probable. But it is surer still that the overthrow of Slavery will at once make an end of the war."

Lincoln had to work with the Radical Republicans in Congress. He appointed some abolitionists to high-ranking positions in the government. But during the first two years of the Civil War, Lincoln maintained that the war was being fought to preserve the Union, not to prohibit slavery.

HOW TO DEAL WITH THE SLAVES

At the start of the war, slaves provided a military advantage to the South. Slaves could be used to support Confederate armies as laborers, building roads and fortifications. Also, their presence working on southern farms allowed more white southerners to fight against the federal military, known as the Union Army. To weaken the South, in 1861 Congress passed a law called the Confiscation Act. It declared that any slave who worked to help the Confederacy would be declared "contraband of war," and given their freedom.

As Union armies moved into the rebellious southern states, tens of thousands of slaves fled from their plantations and sought their protection. Army commanders sometimes enlisted the slaves to work for the Union forces. Other times, they were placed in camps, where starvation and disease led to a high death rate. Abolitionists in the North organized efforts to provide food and medicine for these camps, and organized schools to teach the escaped slaves how to read and write.

After a Union victory at the Battle of Antietam in September 1862, President Lincoln issued the Emancipation Proclamation. According to this order, if the rebellion did not end by January

Runaway slaves cross the Rappahannock River in Virginia, seeking protection from Union troops, July 1862. The government policy was to treat escaped slaves as captured enemy property, or "contrabands."

By the President of the United States of America:

A Proclamation.

Whereas, on the twenty-second day of September, in the year of our Lord one thousand eight hundred and sixty-two, a proclamation was issued by the President of the United States, containing, among other things, the following, to wit:

"That on the first day of January, in the year of our Lord one thousand eight hundred and sixty-three, all persons held as slaves within any State or designated part of a State, the people whereof shall then be in rebellion against the United States, shall be then, thenceforward, and forever free; and the Executive Government of the United States, including the military and naval authority thereof, will recognize and maintain the freedom of such persons, and will do no act or acts to repress such persons, or any of them, in any efforts they may make for their actual freedom.

"That the Executive will, on the first day

The first page of the Emancipation Proclamation, which declared all slaves in the rebellious states free as of January 1, 1863.

1, 1863, all slaves in the rebel areas would become free. The Proclamation did not end slavery in the border states. It only freed slaves in Confederate states where the Union Army did not have control. The proclamation could not be enforced until federal troops regained control of those states.

THE 10 PERCENT PLAN

The Union strategy for winning the war was to gain control over important waterways, like the Mississippi River. At the time, rivers were the fastest way to move supplies from place to place, or to ship products to foreign markets for sale. Controlling the rivers would hurt the Confederacy's economy.

New Orleans, the largest city in the Confederacy, was captured in April 1862. Because of the city's importance as a commercial center, some people there were willing to rejoin the Union so they could continue to trade with other countries.

From New Orleans, Union forces worked their way up the Mississippi and other waterways in the West. By 1863, the federal government had regained control over large areas of Louisiana, Tennessee, and Arkansas.

Before the war, most people in Tennessee had wanted to stay in the Union. But when Lincoln called for troops to put down the rebellion, Tennessee residents voted to secede. Nonetheless, there was still a strong minority that supported the Union cause, especially in the eastern part of the state. By the end of 1863, the Union army controlled most of the state. At the same time, Union forces captured major cities in Arkansas, including Helena and the capital, Little Rock, and controlled most of that state as well.

The question facing Lincoln and the federal government was how to re-integrate citizens of those states into the United States. Lincoln struggled to find the best approach. He eventually settled on an idea that became known as the 10 percent plan. Lincoln's idea was that a southern state could be readmitted into the Union once 10 percent of the state's voters (based on the list

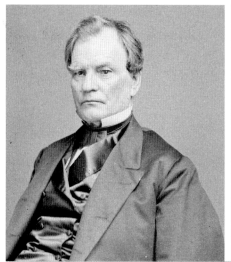

Senator Benjamin F. Wade of Ohio and Congressman Henry W. Davis of Maryland introduced legislation that would punish rebellious states, but their bill failed to become law.

of those who had voted in 1860) swore an Oath of Allegiance to the United States. The state's voters could then elect delegates to a convention, where they would draft a revised state constitution and create a new state government. All residents of the state would be granted a full pardon, except for high-ranking members of the Confederate government and military. The state's residents would be allowed to keep their private property, but not their slaves, because the new state constitutions were required to outlaw slavery.

Lincoln proposed this plan in December 1863, calling it the Proclamation of Amnesty and Reconstruction. Once a state's government was "reconstructed," it would be allowed to send representatives to Congress and participate in national elections. In 1864, Louisiana, Tennessee, and Arkansas began the reconstruction process under Lincoln's 10 percent plan.

However, the Radical Republican faction in Congress thought the 10 percent plan was too easy on the southern rebels. The

Wade-Davis Bill was legislation proposed in Congress that would make it harder for states to be readmitted to the Union. Under the Wade-Davis Bill, 50 percent of voters in the state would have to take the loyalty oath, not just 10 percent. However, Lincoln was able to veto the Wade-Davis Bill, preventing it from becoming law.

ENDING THE WAR, AND ENDING SLAVERY

The Emancipation Proclamation was an important step toward ending slavery. However, because it was simply a presidential order, a future president would have the power to revoke the proclamation and allow slavery again. The only way to permanently eliminate slavery in the United States was through an amendment to the US Constitution. This would ensure that slavery could never again be permitted in the United States.

These campaign buttons from the 1864 presidential election feature portraits of Abraham Lincoln and vice presidential candidate Andrew Johnson.

Before a Constitutional amendment was possible, Lincoln would have to be re-elected as president. Not everyone was happy with the job he was doing, especially during the early years of the war. In 1862 and early 1863 the Union Army had suffered embarrassing defeats at places like Bull Run, Chancellorsville, Fredericksburg, and Shiloh. Some of the Radical Republicans wanted to replace Lincoln with another candidate: John C. Frémont, who had been the party's presidential nominee in 1856. Unless Lincoln gained their support, he might not even be on the ballot in the 1864 election.

However, Union victories on the battlefield during 1863 and 1864 made Americans more confident that Lincoln was leading the nation to victory. Frémont withdrew his name from consideration and supported Lincoln, and the rest of the Republican Party did the same.

The Democratic Party in the North was divided by the war. Some Democrats wanted the government to immediately stop fighting and make peace with the Confederacy. They were called Copperheads. Other Democrats wanted to continue the war and end the rebellion. They were called the "War Democrats." To attract their support, Lincoln chose a War Democrat named Andrew Johnson, who was from Tennessee, to be his vice presidential running mate. Johnson had been the only senator from a Confederate state who did not resign from Congress when the war began. Most War Democrats ended up voting for Lincoln, and he easily won a second term as president. Passage of the Thirteenth Amendment to the US Constitution would become a priority after Lincoln was re-elected.

During four years of war, the Confederate armies had won a few notable victories. However, the federal government had important advantages over the South. The northern states had many more men and greater industrial resources than the southern states did. They could produce more cannons, rifles, and other military material, and provide more soldiers for the fight.

After 1863, black soldiers played an important part in the Union war effort. More than 180,000 black Americans served in the military during the Civil War. By war's end, nearly 40,000 black soldiers had been killed. Sixteen black soldiers were awarded the Medal of Honor, the nation's highest honor, for their courage in battle.

As the Union Army advanced, slaves fled their plantations and sought protection behind their lines. Some of these former slaves were put to work helping the Union Army. Others joined the fight themselves, enlisting in the Union army or navy. By the spring of 1865, it was clear the Confederate states could no longer defend themselves from Union troops.

In his second inaugural address, delivered in March 1865, Lincoln encouraged Americans from both North and South to forgive each other and work together to rebuild the United States: "With malice toward none; with charity for all; with firmness in the right, as God gives us to see the right, let us strive on to finish the work we are in; to bind up the nation's wounds; to care for him who shall have borne the battle, and for his widow, and his orphan—to do all which may achieve and cherish a just, and a lasting peace, among ourselves, and with all nations."

In April 1865, the Union Army captured the Confederate capital at Richmond, Virginia, forcing Jefferson Davis and the Confederate government to flee. A few days later, General Robert E. Lee surrendered what was left of his army at nearby Appomattox Court House. Over the next two months, Confederates kept fighting in a few places, but most recognized that the rebellion was over. Now, a battle over how to make peace between the states would begin in earnest.

Confederate general Robert E. Lee (left) signs the document surrendering his Army of Northern Virginia to Union commander General Ulysses S. Grant on April 9, 1865. Lee's surrender did not end the Civil War—some small groups of Confederates would continue fighting until June of 1865—but it did mark the end of major combat operations by the southern rebels.

1. Why did Lincoln wait until after the Battle of Antietam to issue the Emancipation Proclamation?

2. What were two major effects of the Emancipation Proclamation?

3. What were the terms of Lincoln's 10 percent plan to readmit the rebellious states to the Union?

RESEARCH PROJECT

Using your library and the internet, research the wartime contributions of African Americans during the Civil War, including (but not limited to) spying, sabotage, nursing, or fighting in the army. Choose an individual and write a three-page report detailing that person's participation in the war and evaluating the importance of their actions.

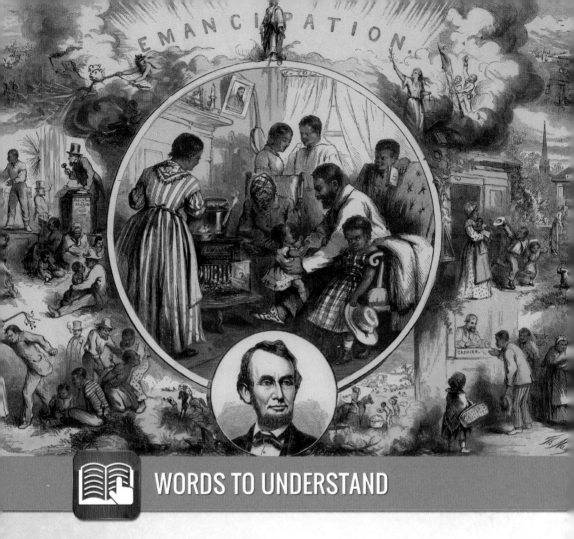

WORDS TO UNDERSTAND

When something has been **nullified**, it is no longer in force or active; it has been canceled out.

A **punitive** approach is one that is intended to punish someone for wrongdoing.

To **ratify** something means to give it formal approval or consent. When amending the US Constitution, state legislatures, which represent the citizens of their state, must vote to ratify the amendment.

A **sympathizer** is someone who agrees with or supports a particular idea of cause.

CHAPTER 2

The Thirteenth Amendment

By the time the Civil War ended, the Thirteenth Amendment was already well on its way to becoming part of the US Constitution. The Constitution includes a process that allows amendments, or changes, to be made. First, two-thirds of the members of both houses of Congress have to approve the wording of an amendment. Then, three-quarters of the states must vote to **ratify** the amendment. Once this happens, the amendment becomes part of the Constitution—the law of the land.

The Thirteenth Amendment was passed by the Senate in April 1864, and by the House of Representatives in January 1865. But ratification by the states posed a potential problem. There had been thirty-four states when the Civil War began, and two states (West Virginia and Nevada) were added during the conflict, bringing the total to thirty-six. That meant twenty-seven of the states had to ratify the Thirteenth Amendment for it to go into effect. To reach that number, at least two of the rebellious

Opposite page: An 1865 illustration by Thomas Nast celebrates ratification of the Thirteenth Amendment. The illustrations on the left show scenes of slavery, and on the right scenes of freedom, including black children attending public schools and black workers being paid for their labor.

states that had joined the Confederacy would have to ratify the amendment, along with all twenty-five states that had remained loyal to the Union during the war.

Within a month after the amendment was passed by both houses of Congress, many of the northern states had voted on it. By early March, eighteen of the northern states had ratified the amendment. However, the legislatures in three Union states—the slave-holding border states of Delaware and Kentucky, as well as New Jersey—had rejected the Thirteenth Amendment. The amendment faced an uphill battle unless the southern states could be brought back into the government.

RATIFICATION BY "RECONSTRUCTED" STATES

With the war over, federal authorities had to figure out the best way to re-integrate the rebellious southern states back into the United States. Lincoln addressed this problem in his last public speech, which he gave a few days after the Confederate surrender at Appomattox. "We all agree that the seceded States, so called, are out of their proper relation with the Union; and that the sole object of the government, civil and military, in regard to those States is to again get them into that proper practical relation," he said.

"Reconstruction" was the term that Lincoln used for the process of returning the southern states to their "proper practical relation" with the national government.

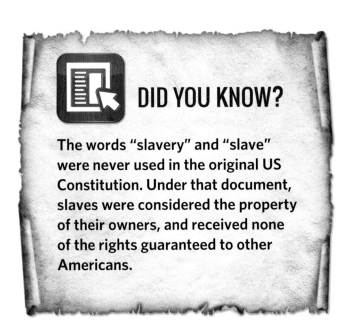

DID YOU KNOW?

The words "slavery" and "slave" were never used in the original US Constitution. Under that document, slaves were considered the property of their owners, and received none of the rights guaranteed to other Americans.

To help newly freed slaves, as well as poor whites, in the devastated post-war South, President Lincoln created a government agency called the Freedmen's Bureau. This 1865 cartoon depicts the agency's leader, Union General Oliver O. Howard, mediating between angry whites and blacks.

In the same speech, Lincoln acknowledged that "the re-inauguration of the national authority—reconstruction—which has had a large share of thought from the first, is ... fraught with great difficulty." The difficulty involved the continuing disagreement between the moderates, led by Lincoln, and the Radical Republican faction in Congress over how reconstruction should be carried out.

Lincoln had clearly expressed his own feelings about how federal authorities should treat the defeated South: "Let 'em up easy." It was a philosophy he had developed as a young man competing in wrestling contests on the frontier—he found that when he defeated someone, the opponent would respect and appreciate being shown mercy. Through Lincoln's 10 percent plan, Louisiana, Arkansas, and Tennessee had already set up

On the evening of April 14, 1865, President Lincoln and his wife Mary attended a play at Ford's Theater in Washington, D.C. Shortly after 10 PM, an actor and Confederate sympathizer named John Wilkes Booth quietly entered the box where the Lincolns were sitting with some friends. He shot Lincoln in the back of the head, then jumped from the box onto the stage and escaped.

The president was carried across the street, to Petersen's Boarding House. A doctor in the audience helped Lincoln as much as possible, but there was little that could be done. The bullet had passed through Lincoln's brain, and he was in a coma. Lincoln died around 7:22 AM the next morning.

The assassination of President Lincoln was part of a larger plot. Booth had sent friends to kill two other important US government officials, Vice President Andrew Johnson and Secretary of State William H. Seward. All three of the attacks were supposed to take place at the same time. However, the other two attacks failed.

A reward was offered for Booth and his accomplices. Many people were arrested, and Booth was killed by Union soldiers. Ultimately, eight people were convicted of involvement in the plot. Four were hanged; the others were imprisoned.

No one knows exactly what John Wilkes Booth hoped to gain by killing the president. Booth hated the idea that blacks would be equal to whites, and may have thought killing the leaders of the US government would create confusion that would give the collapsing Confederacy a chance to regroup. However, the assassination did not help the South. The war was already decided, and Lincoln's death angered northerners, enabling the Radical Republicans to impose tougher restrictions on the southern states.

"reconstructed" governments. The new state legislatures in those states voted on the Thirteenth Amendment in the spring of 1865. Louisiana ratified the amendment on February 17, Tennessee on April 7, and Arkansas on April 14.

Tragically, Lincoln probably never heard the news about Arkansas's ratification of the Thirteenth Amendment. That night, he was shot in Washington, D.C., while attending the theater with his wife. Lincoln died early the next morning.

JOHNSON'S PRESIDENTIAL RECONSTRUCTION

Lincoln's assassination shocked the nation. In April of 1865, with the war ended, many Americans considered the president a hero who had saved the nation from division. Lincoln had been able to use his popularity to build support for the Thirteenth Amendment. Without Lincoln to push the matter, some abolitionists feared that the pace of ratification would stall. Lincoln had also been able to

A nineteenth-century illustration shows John Wilkes Booth shooting President Lincoln in the back of the head, April 14, 1865.

outmaneuver the Radical Republican congressmen who wanted to punish the South for the Civil War. If Lincoln had lived, the history of post-war reconstruction, and of the United States, might have been very different.

After Lincoln's death, Vice President Andrew Johnson became president. Like Lincoln, Johnson did not want to put many obstacles in the way of reconstructing the former Confederate states. Both men believed that re-integrating the rebellious states into the Union would help to heal the wounds of the Civil War. But Johnson was different in several important respects. Johnson had been a slave owner. He did not believe that blacks were equal to whites. Like other northern Democrats he did not want to see blacks receive the rights of citizenship, including the right to vote.

These attitudes would bring President Johnson into heated conflict with the Radical Republicans in Congress. They wanted to take a more **punitive** approach to the southern states, which they blamed for starting the war. They also wanted to protect the rights of the newly freed black slaves in the South, and ensure that the slave system could never emerge again.

However, Congress was not due to meet until December 1865, so for about eight months President Johnson was in charge of

Scan here to learn more about Andrew Johnson's attitude toward black Americans.

A slaveowner before the Civil War, Andrew Johnson claimed in 1863 that his attitude toward slavery had changed, and he granted his slaves freedom. In 1864, as military governor of Tennessee, Johnson issued an order freeing all slaves in the state. However, as president, Johnson tried to block legislation that would give blacks the same rights as white Americans.

the reconstruction effort. He appointed governors to oversee reconstruction in many of the rebellious states. The governors made sure that people took the loyalty oath and held elections to create new state legislatures.

Johnson offered a pardon to all southern whites, other than high-ranking Confederate leaders and the wealthiest plantation owners. He restored the southerners' voting rights as well as all of their property, except for their slaves. Many people who had supported the Confederacy could therefore vote for members of the new state governments. They could even serve in the legislatures if elected.

Under Johnson's plan, southern states were required to ratify the Thirteenth Amendment. The Confederate government had borrowed money from other countries to help pay for the Civil War, so the former Confederate states also had to agree to pay a share of these war debts. When a state met these conditions, Johnson intended to allow the state government to manage its own affairs—including the question of which state residents would be allowed to vote.

The Thirteenth Amendment continued to make progress through the state legislatures. Ratifications by Connecticut on

The Freedmen's Bureau operated schools to teach former slaves how to read and write, such as this one pictured in Virginia. The Bureau also provided food for people who were too sick or old to work, both black and white, and established refugee camps for those who had lost their homes during the war.

May 4 and New Hampshire on July 1 brought the total to twenty-three states. Four were still needed. South Carolina ratified the amendment on November 13, followed by Alabama on December 2, North Carolina on December 4, and Georgia on December 6. On December 18, 1865, the US Secretary of State William H. Seward certified that the Thirteenth Amendment had become part of the Constitution.

The Thirteenth Amendment abolished slavery and involuntary, or forced, servitude for anyone in the United States. The only exception would be in the case of convicted criminals who were sentenced to work for the state as part of their punishment. The amendment gave Congress the authority to pass laws that would protect people from becoming slaves.

PROBLEMS WITH PRESIDENTIAL RECONSTRUCTION

When it was passed, the Thirteenth Amendment **nullified** the "three-fifths compromise" of the original Constitution. This was a provision in Article 1, Section 2 of the Constitution for calculating the number of representatives that each state would send to Congress. Membership in the House of Representatives was based on population, with more populous states having a greater number of representatives. Under the original Constitution, a state's population would include all free persons, plus "three-fifths of all other persons" residing in that state. Therefore, before 1865 each slave was counted as three-fifths of a free person.

After passage of the Thirteenth Amendment, each former slave would count the same as every white person. There were about 4 million newly freed slaves living in the southern states, so that would change the balance of power in the House

A copy of the Oath of Allegiance, signed by a former Confederate soldier from North Carolina named Andrew J. P. Giddings in November 1865.

of Representatives. The southern states would gain more representatives, while the states of the north and west would lose representatives in Congress.

Republicans in Congress expected that if the freedmen were allowed to vote, they would support Republican candidates. After all, the Republicans were Lincoln's party and had provided slaves the pathway to emancipation. The Democratic Party, on the other hand, was largely made up of planters and former slave owners. It was the party of states' rights, and the dominant party in the South before the secession crisis.

But whether the freedmen would be allowed to vote was a different matter. The Constitution did not define which Americans were eligible to vote, or how elections for federal, state, or local government officials should be held. It was left up to each state's legislature to establish its own requirements for voting and the procedures for electing public officials.

Because President Johnson had allowed the reconstructed states to manage their own affairs, the new state legislatures were dominated by white Democrats, many of whom were former Confederates. They did not want freedmen to vote, or have any of the rights that whites did. The new southern state governments prepared to do what was needed to rebuild the South's economy and keep whites in control of the newly freed black population.

1. How many state legislatures had to ratify the Thirteenth Amendment for it to become part of the US Constitution?

2. Why did President Johnson, not Congress, oversee the first eight months of reconstruction?

3. What advantage would the South receive when the "three-fifths clause" was nullified?

RESEARCH PROJECT

Using the internet or a library, research the Thirteenth, Fourteenth, and Fifteenth amendments. Who proposed these amendments, and how much opposition did they face? What led to the amendments getting passed in such a turbulent time in history? Do you think that there would still be segregation today if these amendments had not passed? Why or why not?

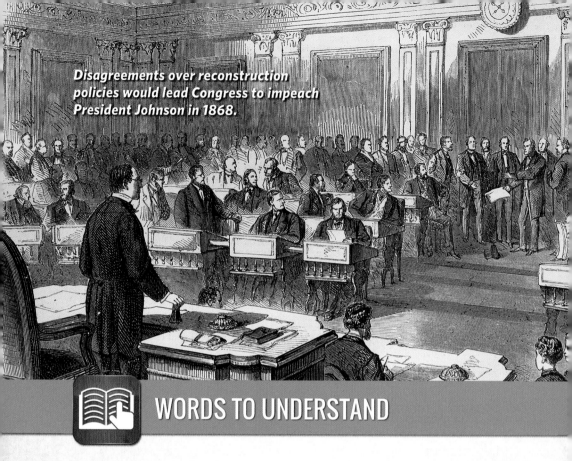

Disagreements over reconstruction policies would lead Congress to impeach President Johnson in 1868.

WORDS TO UNDERSTAND

A **cash crop** is an agricultural product that is produced because it is easy to sell, instead of for consumption by the farmer and his or her family. Tobacco, cotton, and rice were important cash crops in the South at the time of the Civil War.

Rule by a military, rather than civilian, government is known as **martial law**.

When someone feels a duty or commitment to do something, they are said to have an **obligation**.

Vagrancy is the condition of being homeless, or unable to support oneself with a job.

The Constitution gives the president the power to **veto**, or block, legislation that the president does not agree with. However, if the law passes again by a two-thirds majority in both houses of Congress, this **overrides** the veto and the bill becomes a law despite the president's objection.

CHAPTER 3

The Battle over State Legislatures

The Civil War and passage of the Thirteenth Amendment threatened to destroy the economic system of the South. Without slave labor, there were not enough workers willing to harvest the **cash crops** that the South's economy depended on, such as cotton, rice, or tobacco on the large plantations. Cotton was by far the most profitable crop produced in the South. The new state legislatures in the southern states needed to find a way to keep blacks toiling in the cotton fields.

To do this, during 1865 and 1866 many southern states enacted new laws that regulated what freed slaves could do. These laws were known as Black Codes. They were intended to replace the old slave system with a new system that would have the same effect.

THE BLACK CODES

Black Codes were nothing new. Laws that regulated the activities of free blacks, as well as slaves, had been passed in many of the American colonies before the American Revolution. Marriage between blacks and whites was illegal, and blacks could not receive gifts, donations, or property from whites. Free blacks had no right to vote in elections, and many public spaces were off-limits to black people. Additionally, blacks could not testify in court against white people, bear arms, assemble in groups, or exercise the free

Former Confederates take the oath of allegiance after the Civil War. Once they had done so, these rebels were permitted to vote in elections and hold public office.

speech rights enjoyed by whites. Before the Civil War, if a black slave was freed in the South, most states required that freedman to leave the state within a few months.

After the Civil War, the southern state legislatures simply updated the old Black Codes to reflect the new post-slavery world. Some of the new Codes prevented blacks from moving away from the plantations where they had lived in slavery. Other codes forced blacks to sign one-year work contracts, which they were not permitted to break, or to work for such low wages that they would never get out of debt. There were rules and regulations about where blacks could settle, marry, or own property. These codes created a system that was little better than slavery—certainly not what Lincoln and other Republican leaders had intended for blacks when they were freed.

In fact, in some ways the new system was even worse than slavery had been. When blacks had been slaves, the white plantation owners had an **obligation** to feed, clothe, and house their slaves. Slaves were property, so keeping them healthy was a worthwhile investment. But after slavery ended the plantation owners no longer felt obligated to do this. The free blacks had to fend for themselves. If a worker became sick, the white landowners would simply hire another worker for the unfairly low wages that the Black Codes permitted, and the sick worker would have to pay a fine for not fulfilling his or her labor contract.

Laws against **vagrancy** were an important aspect of the Black Codes. Some states required blacks to show local officials proof that they were employed on a regular basis. Freedmen who refused to sign the labor contract with the plantation owner could be arrested as vagrants. As punishment for vagrancy, they would be sentenced to a term of involuntary servitude and auctioned off to a white planter. Other laws allowed black people to be arrested for very minor infractions. Like the vagrancy laws, the punishments for these crimes often required them to work without pay for whites.

To learn more about the Black Codes, scan here.

Vagrancy laws were an important element of the Black Codes, allowing authorities to arrest anyone who did not have a job and sentence them to work for a white employer. This image shows a freedman in Monticello, Florida, being auctioned for vagrancy.

Black codes were not limited to the South. Some northern states passed their own Black Codes at this time. They were generally not as severe as the laws in the South, but northerners did not welcome the freedmen, either. This was particularly true in the border states. Blacks who moved North from other states often had a hard time finding enough work to feed themselves or support a family.

CONGRESS TAKES OVER RECONSTRUCTION

The Radical Republicans in the US Congress were upset and angry about the president's reconstruction plan. When Congress convened in December of 1865, it refused to seat the congressmen who had been elected from the southern states.

The next few years saw significant battles in the federal legislature. The Republican Party had a majority in both the Senate and the House of Representatives. Under their leadership, Congress gradually took control over reconstruction. They passed new laws to protect the rights of black Americans in the South. Johnson tried to **veto** the laws, but there were enough Republicans in Congress to **override** the president's vetoes.

One of the first clashes came in February of 1866, when Congress voted to extend the mission of the Freedmen's Bureau. This government agency had been formed to help former slaves and refugees in the South after the Civil War. Johnson vetoed the bill because he felt the legislation infringed on states' rights. He argued that the states, not a federal agency, should be responsible for ensuring the rights of its residents. Republicans refused to let the issue die. Congress voted on the bill again, passing the legislation by a two-thirds majority to override the president's veto and preserve the Freedmen's Bureau.

In March 1866, Congress voted on another bill intended to protect freedmen. The Civil Rights Act of 1866 said that black Americans were citizens of the United States, and deserved the same rights as white Americans. Again, Johnson vetoed the act. In April 1866, Congress again overrode the president's veto.

In June 1866, a Congressional Committee on Reconstruction determined that when the southern states seceded, they had forfeited "all civil and political rights under the Constitution." The Committee rejected Johnson's reconstruction plan, and declared that only Congress could determine how southern states would be re-admitted to the Union.

THE FOURTEENTH AMENDMENT

Congressional leaders recognized that the protections of the Civil Rights Act of 1866 could be eliminated by future lawmakers. And

THE FREEDMEN'S BUREAU

As the Civil War drew to an end, the South was shattered. Cities, towns, and the region's plantation-based economy had been destroyed. Millions of black slaves had been freed, but they lacked the education and resources they would need to fend for themselves. Many former slaves and poor whites were dislocated from their homes and facing starvation.

In March 1865, President Lincoln ordered the creation of a new government agency, called the Bureau of Refugees, Freedmen, and Abandoned Lands, to help rebuild southern society. The Freedmen's Bureau, as it became known, provided assistance to former slaves and impoverished whites in the southern states and the District of Columbia. It issued food and clothing, and operated hospitals, schools, and temporary camps for displaced refugees. The Freedmen's Bureau also helped to reunite black families by finding missing members, and enabled freed slaves to legalize their marriages. Through the efforts of the Freedmen's Bureau, former slaves were settled on abandoned or confiscated lands. The Bureau also tried to create a new economic system in which the former slaves would be fairly paid for their work on cotton plantations. It investigated racial confrontations and provided legal representation when needed.

The Freedmen's Bureau was originally intended to operate for a year, so that former slaves could transition to freedom. However, the Black Codes in the South led Congress to extend the mission of the Bureau. Although the Freedmen's Bureau tried to protect the rights of blacks in the South, it was opposed by President Johnson, who argued that its work infringed on the rights of the state governments. In 1872, due to growing opposition from southerners in Congress, the Freedmen's Bureau was closed down.

the feared that the southern states, once readmitted to the Union, would have enough representatives to make that happen. The only way to ensure those rights were protected was to guarantee them in the US Constitution.

Republicans in Congress soon drafted the Fourteenth Amendment. It declared that blacks who had been born in the United States were Americans citizens, and said that states could not deny anyone equal protection under the law because of their race. This overturned a controversial US Supreme Court decision, *Dred Scott v. Sanford* (1857), which had determined that blacks could not be citizens. The amendment also prevented former Confederates from serving in the state or federal government, and declared that the United States would not be responsible for paying the Confederate war debt. The Fourteenth Amendment was passed by Congress in June 1866.

The new Congressional plan for reconstruction required new state legislatures to be formed in the eleven former Confederate states. To be re-admitted to the Union, the legislatures would have to write new constitutions that allowed black men to vote, and ratify the Fourteenth Amendment.

President Johnson encouraged the southern states not to vote for the amendment. Ten of the eleven former Confederate states refused to ratify the amendment; the only exception was Tennessee. Johnson supported Democratic candidates in the 1866 Congressional election, but Republicans won most of the seats in the House of Representatives and Senate.

With a solid Republican majority, in March 1867 Congress again overrode a presidential veto in order to pass the Military Reconstruction Act. This legislation divided the South (other than Tennessee) into five military districts. Each district would be controlled by a Union general and his troops, who had the power to maintain order and protect the civil rights of free blacks. To end this period of **martial law**, the southern states had to meet Congress's previously stated conditions on reconstruction: ratify the Fourteenth Amendment and adopt new state constitutions that gave blacks the right to vote.

IMPEACHMENT

President Johnson continued trying to thwart the Radical Republicans, but Congress simply passed the bills over his veto. In March of 1868, the House of Representatives drew up charges of impeachment against the president. This was the first time in American history that a president had been impeached. A trial was held in the Senate, with senators from twenty-six Union states plus Tennessee participating. At the end of the trial, the fifty-four senators voted on three of the charges. On each charge, 35 senators found Johnson guilty, while 19 voted to acquit Johnson of the charges.

Although most senators voted to impeach Johnson, they were one vote short of the two-thirds majority that the Constitution required to actually remove the president from office. Johnson remained, but had little ability to affect the reconstruction process. He did not run for reelection in 1868. The Republican Party nominated Civil War hero Ulysses S. Grant as its candidate. Grant easily won a majority in the electoral college—thanks in part to the votes of approximately 500,000 freedmen who were permitted to participate in a presidential election for the first time.

TEXT-DEPENDENT QUESTIONS

1. Why were the black codes worse than slavery in some ways?

2. What was the punishment for freedmen who were found guilty of violating vagrancy laws?

3. What was the purpose of the Freedmen's Bureau?

4. How did the Military Reconstruction Act of 1867 change the pace of postwar reconstruction?

RESEARCH PROJECT

Andrew Johnson was the first US president to be impeached, or accused of abusing his office. Using your school library or the internet, find out more about the impeachment process, which is detailed in Article One of the US Constitution. Write a two-page paper explaining the crimes for which a president can be impeached, the steps that must be taken to begin an impeachment proceeding, and the trial process in the Senate.

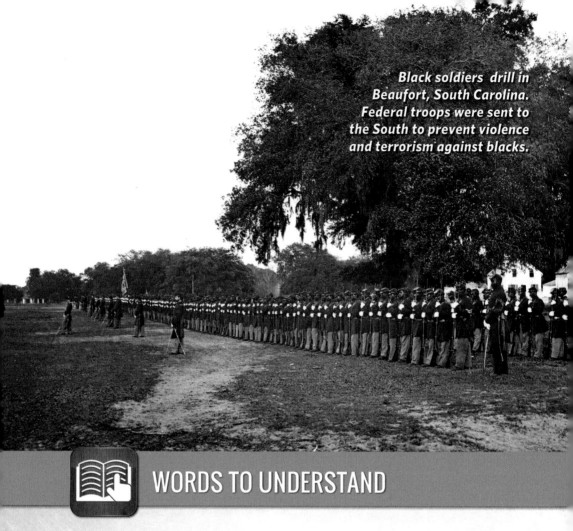

Black soldiers drill in Beaufort, South Carolina. Federal troops were sent to the South to prevent violence and terrorism against blacks.

WORDS TO UNDERSTAND

A person from the northern states who moved to the South after the Civil War to help with reconstruction was known as a **carpetbagger**. (The term refers to an inexpensive suitcase.) This was an insulting term; southerners saw carpetbaggers as opportunists who wanted to profit from their misfortunes.

When groups of people work together for a common purpose, they can be said to have formed a **coalition**.

An **economic depression** is a period when the nation's business and trade activity is sharply reduced.

A white southerner who benefited from collaborating with Republicans and carpetbaggers during reconstruction was mockingly called a **scalawag**.

CHAPTER 4

The Fifteenth Amendment and the Force Acts

At the time of the Civil War, only white men were allowed to vote in most states. Beginning in 1867, Congress's reconstruction legislation enabled black men to vote in most of the southern states. However, some northern states still did not allow free blacks to vote, and future laws could reverse black voting rights in the South. So Congress set out to guarantee the voting rights of all black Americans by passing another amendment to the Constitution.

The Fifteenth Amendment said that no US citizen could be denied the right to vote because of his race or because he had previously been a slave. Congress passed the Fifteenth Amendment in 1869 and it was ratified by the states in 1870.

Republican Party leaders expected that black voters would support the party in elections, because of their support for ending slavery and protecting black Americans' rights. Blacks did vote overwhelmingly for Republican candidates, but some white southerners also supported the Republican Party. Often, they were businessmen who stood to benefit personally from the restoration of trade and commerce between the North and the South, or those who had not been slaveowners before the war. These people were criticized by southern whites, who called them **scalawags** because they did not support the traditional values of the South—including

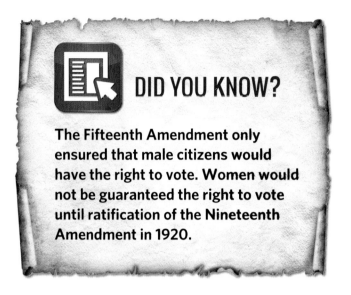

DID YOU KNOW?

The Fifteenth Amendment only ensured that male citizens would have the right to vote. Women would not be guaranteed the right to vote until ratification of the Nineteenth Amendment in 1920.

the belief that whites were superior to blacks.

In addition, between 1865 and 1870 tens of thousands of northerners traveled to the South to help the Freedmen's Bureau with reconstruction efforts. They worked as teachers, doctors, lawyers, or government bureaucrats, and generally voted Republican as well. Most whites in the South looked down on these northerners, calling them **carpetbaggers**. They believed that the northerners were opportunists who had come to profit from the South's problems.

Due to this **coalition** of black and white voters, the Republican Party dominated southern legislatures between 1868 and 1877. An unprecedented number of blacks were elected to local, state, or federal offices from the southern states. One of them was Hiram Revels, a Mississippi state legislator who in February of 1870 became the first African American to serve in the US Senate.

A few months later, Joseph Rainey of South Carolina became the first black man elected to serve in the US House of Representatives. As a Congressman, Rainey tried to protect the rights of black Americans. "I tell you that the Negro will never rest until he gets his rights," he said. "We ask [for civil rights] because

Opposite: The cover of Harper's Weekly, *a popular magazine, shows a line of black American men lined up to participate in an election in 1867. The first is dressed as a laborer casting his vote. The second man appears to be a businessman, the third is wearing a Union Army uniform, and the fourth is dressed as a farmer.*

HARPER'S WEEKLY.

A JOURNAL OF CIVILIZATION.

VOL. XI.—No. 568.]   NEW YORK, SATURDAY, NOVEMBER 16, 1867.   [SINGLE COPIES TEN CENTS.
[$4.00 PER YEAR IN ADVANCE.

Entered according to Act of Congress, in the Year 1867, by Harper & Brothers, in the Clerk's Office of the District Court for the Southern District of New York.

"THE FIRST VOTE."—DRAWN BY A. R. WAUD.—[SEE NEXT PAGE.]

The first black American members of Congress included (front, left to right) Senator Hiram R. Revels of Mississippi, Benjamin S. Turner of Alabama, Josiah T. Walls of Florida, Joseph H. Rainey and R. Brown Elliot of South Carolina, (back) Robert C. De Large of South Carolina, and Jefferson H. Long of Georgia. All were elected as Republicans.

we know it is proper, not because we want to deprive any other class of the rights and immunities they enjoy, but because they are granted to us by the law of the land." Rainey was re-elected to Congress four times, serving until March 3, 1879. No other black American would serve as long in Congress until the 1950s.

VIOLENT BACKLASH

While some people worked to unify blacks and whites, others in the South were firmly opposed to equality. Instead, they wanted blacks kept "in their place"—oppressed and under the control of whites, as they had been during slavery. Groups of former Confederates began to organize in an attempt to prevent black equality and combat the work of Republican-controlled governments.

The most infamous of these groups was the Ku Klux Klan (KKK), which was founded by six Confederate veterans in 1865 in Pulaski, Tennessee. The name is taken from the Greek word for circle, *kuklos*. Most accounts indicate that the group was originally formed for benign purposes, as a social club. However, with the enfranchisement of black voters in 1867 the Klan became a violent hate group that terrorized those who threatened white power throughout the South.

The hooded disguises of Klan night riders struck terror in the hearts of citizens throughout the South. Klan members threatened, whipped, and murdered both blacks and whites who supported equal rights for African Americans. Black people were the Klan's main target—especially educators and ministers who tried to better the lives of former slaves. Black churches, schools, businesses, and homes were often burned. Lynchings were intended to send a message to other blacks about the danger of voting for Republicans or interfering with white rule in the South.

The Klan and other white supremacist groups, like the Red Shirts and the White League, were openly associated with the

To find out more about white supremacy today, scan here.

A Ku Klux Klansman aims his rifle into an African-American home. The menace of the Klan made many blacks afraid to vote.

Democratic Party in the South. In Georgia, Klan members created a group called the Young Men's Democratic Society to influence the state elections during 1868. By day, members of the Society denounced Republican candidates and encouraged people to vote for Democrats. At night, Society members donned their Klan robes and terrorized the countryside. The Klan murdered more than 330 people in Georgia during the months leading up to the election.

Blacks and whites were scared, and this was reflected in the election returns in November 1868. Counties where more than a thousand people had voted for the Republican candidate in April of 1868 saw just over 100 voting for Republicans in November. In Columbia County, there was only one Republican vote cast in the November election. As a result, Democrats won a majority of seats in the new Georgia legislature.

Blacks in Georgia and elsewhere refused to be beaten into submission. They rebuilt their churches and schools. They armed themselves and fought back when their communities were threatened.

THE FORCE ACTS

Though the Ku Klux Klan was formidable, its power quickly began to wane after 1870. That is because the Republican-controlled Congress quickly took action. The Civil Rights Act of 1870, also called the Force Act, authorized the president to send the army to areas where the KKK and other groups were using terrorism to suppress the black vote. Additional laws were passed in 1871, giving federal authorities the ability to penalize individuals or organizations that tried to prevent blacks from registering to vote or voting in elections, holding public office, serving on juries, or otherwise participating in society. The laws created federal election supervisors who would make sure that southern elections were fair.

The Grant administration was willing to send troops to enforce the law. In 1871 and 1872, more than 5,000 southerners were indicted for violating the civil rights of blacks. The Force Acts broke the power of the Ku Klux Klan Acts, sharply reducing the violence against freedmen, although it did not disappear completely.

Enforcing the law and eliminating groups like the KKK could not change the way people felt in their hearts. Interventions by federal troops made southerners angry and resentful toward northerners and black Americans. White state officials still wanted

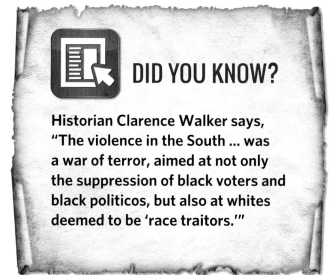

DID YOU KNOW?

Historian Clarence Walker says, "The violence in the South ... was a war of terror, aimed at not only the suppression of black voters and black politicos, but also at whites deemed to be 'race traitors.'"

to keep blacks down, and often sought loopholes in the law that would enable them to limit the rights of blacks. And while the KKK was weakened, other groups would be formed to fill the void.

GROWING OPPOSITION TO RECONSTRUCTION

White Democrats in the South were not the only people opposed to Republican reconstruction policies. Grant's administration was widely criticized due to its corruption. Most historians agree that the president was personally honest. However, many people that Grant appointed to government positions were willing to use their political power to enrich themselves and their friends. One of the scandals—an 1869 attempt by some Wall Street financiers to manipulate the price of gold—damaged the national economy and caused the price of farm products to fall. Others involved Grant appointees accepting bribes in return for political favors. Republican congressmen, and even Grant's vice president, were implicated in these scandals.

Many people in both the North and South grew increasingly suspicious of continued Republican rule. Southerners claimed that the Grant administration was using its power to make sure that Republicans won elections in the South. They accused the administration of prolonging reconstruction to ensure that Republicans would stay in power nationally.

By 1872, even some Republicans started to believe that reconstruction had lasted for too long. They included Senator Lyman Trumbull of Illinois, who had helped to write the Thirteenth Amendment. Trumbull came to believe that the continued presence of US troops did more to antagonize southern whites than it did to help freedmen. Another was Senator Charles Sumner of Massachusetts, who had been one of the leading anti-slavery advocates in Congress. In 1866, Sumner had pushed the Radical Republicans' plan for reconstruction through Congress. But by 1872, he agreed with Trumbull that Grant's approach to reconstruction was not working.

Armed white men retreat in the moonlit night after shooting three blacks near Trenton, Tennessee, in 1874. The number of attacks on black Americans increased in the 1870s, despite federal laws.

In 1872 Trumbull and Sumner formed a new party, the Liberal Republican Party, to challenge Grant in the presidential election. The Liberal Republicans nominated New York newspaper editor Horace Greeley as their candidate.

The Democratic Party also endorsed Greeley as their candidate. Party leaders wanted to unite anti-Grant voters behind a single candidate, as that was their best strategy to defeat the incumbent president. However, many Democrats were not enthusiastic about

Greeley, who for many years had been a prominent critic of slavery and the Democratic Party. Grant wound up winning a second term as president, with about 56 percent of the vote.

Nonetheless, Republican control over the federal government was weakening. An **economic depression** that began in 1873 caused more voters to turn to the Democratic Party in state and local elections. Democratic supporters resorted to their old tactics of using violence and intimidation to prevent blacks from voting, and the Democrats gained control of more state and local governments.

In 1873, Republicans and Democrats in Louisiana disputed the election for governor. In April 1873 a mob of Democrats attacked Republicans at the courthouse in Colfax, Louisiana, killing over 150 blacks. Federal prosecutors used the Force Act to charge several white men with the murders. However, the Supreme Court ruled in *United States v. Cruikshank* that the legislation did not apply to individual acts. The Court opinion said that states, not the federal government, were responsible for protecting black rights. This ruling made it impossible for the federal government to use to Force Act to punish those who violated black civil rights. The Louisiana state government, which was now controlled by the Democratic Party, refused to bring charges against the white men who had been involved in the Colfax massacre.

With the public tiring of reconstruction, Grant was reluctant to continue sending troops to protect the freedmens' rights or to support Republican officeholders in the South. In 1875 Congress passed a new Civil Rights Act that prohibited discrimination in transportation, restaurants, and theaters. Grant signed the law, but did not instruct federal authorities to enforce it.

Across the nation, the tide was turning against reconstruction. In 1874, nearly half of the Republican congressmen were swept from power and Democrats gained control of the House of Representatives for the first time since the Civil War. The end of the Reconstruction Era was fast approaching.

TEXT-DEPENDENT QUESTIONS

1. Who was the first black American to serve in Congress?
2. How did the Ku Klux Klan and other groups prevent blacks from voting?
3. What Republican congressmen formed the Liberal Republican Party to challenge President Grant in 1872?

RESEARCH PROJECT

Using your school library or the internet, take a closer look at the Force Acts and presidential authority. Do you think it is a good idea for the president to have this kind of authority? Why or why not? In other circumstances or situations, are there ways in which having this kind of power might lead to an abuse of that power? Can you give an example?

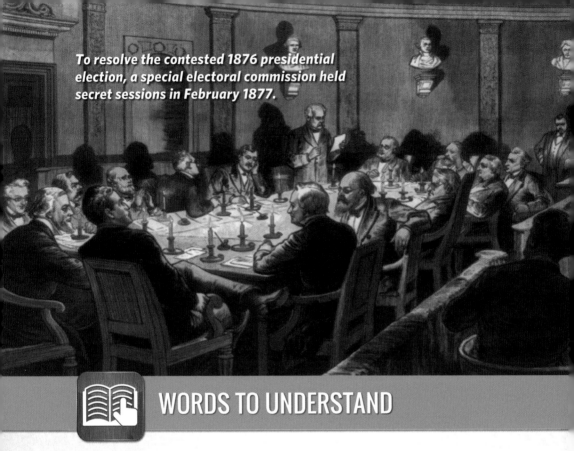

To resolve the contested 1876 presidential election, a special electoral commission held secret sessions in February 1877.

WORDS TO UNDERSTAND

To perform in **blackface** means for a white actor or entertainer to wear makeup and pretend to be a black person. During the nineteenth and early twentieth century, minstrel show entertainers made fun of black Americans by acting out stereotypes wearing blackface makeup. Today, blackface portrayals are considered very offensive and disrespectful.

To **disenfranchise** someone means to take away their right to vote in elections and participate in civic life.

When an election is **disputed,** there is an disagreement over whether the results of voting are fair or valid.

The **Redeemers** were white southerners who came to power at the end of the Reconstruction Era, and dominated politics in the South until the early twentieth century. Many had been part of wealthy slaveowning families, and they implemented policies to ensure that white supremacy would continue.

CHAPTER 5

The End of Reconstruction

Reconstruction could not go on forever, and the presidential election in 1876 marked the end. The campaign between the Republican candidate, Rutherford B. Hayes, and the Democratic candidate, Samuel J. Tilden, was among the most controversial, contested, and hostile in United States history.

Tilden won about 51 percent of the total votes cast, while Hayes received about 48 percent. However, the country does not elect leaders based on the popular vote. Instead, it uses the Electoral College. Each state selects a number of electors equal to the number of representatives it sent to Congress. If a majority of voters in a state voted for the Democratic candidate, all of the electors from that state would be Democrats. If a majority supported the Republican candidate, all the state's electors would be Republicans.

When the votes were counted, Tilden had received 184 electoral votes while Hayes had 165. However, twenty electoral votes were **disputed**. If all were awarded to the Republican candidate, it would be enough to make Hayes the winner with 185 electoral votes.

Nineteen of the disputed electoral votes were from the states of Florida (four votes), South Carolina (eight), and Louisiana (seven). When the votes were originally counted, the Democrats appeared to have won a majority in all three states. However,

Republican Rutherford B. Hayes (left) was an abolitionist attorney who had defended fugitive slaves in court before the Civil War and had served as an officer in the Union Army and as governor of Ohio. The Democratic candidate, Samuel J. Tilden (right), was governor of New York at the time of the presidential election. Prior to the Civil War, Tilden had been part of a Democratic Party faction that opposed the spread of slavery into new territories.

they had used fraud and intimidation to win in Florida, South Carolina, and Louisiana. The Republican governor of each state ordered the ballots to be reviewed. When the fraudulent ballots were eliminated, Hayes had a majority. Democrats argued that the Republicans in those states were trying to steal the election.

In Oregon, the Republicans had won the state but the state's Democratic governor dismissed one of the three Republican electors and replaced him with a Democrat, who voted for Tilden. The Republican-controlled Oregon state legislature challenged this move, saying that all three of the state's electoral votes should be awarded to the Republican candidate, Hayes.

A Special Elections Commission was created by Congress in order to examine the situation in these four states, and determine whether the disputed electoral votes should be awarded to Tilden or Hayes. The Commission included five members of the House of Representatives, five Senators, and five Supreme Court justices. Seven members were Republicans, seven were Democrats, and Supreme Court Justice Joseph P. Bradley was considered a political independent.

As inauguration day approached, the country waited to hear who the next president would be. Finally, just two days before the official inauguration day, the Commission awarded all twenty disputed electoral votes to Hayes, by a vote of eight to seven. Hayes was named the president.

A SECRET COMPROMISE?

Today, some historians believe that Republicans and Democrats made a secret deal, called the Compromise of 1877, to settle the issue. They contend that Republicans agreed to remove the last federal troops from the South as long as Democrats in Congress did not protest against awarding the disputed electoral votes to Hayes. Others say that there was no formal agreement, as Hayes had promised to withdraw the troops during his campaign.

To learn more about the election of 1876, scan here.

DID YOU KNOW?

Racial discrimination was not confined to the South during the years after reconstruction ended. Most people did not want blacks to come North. Industrialists preferred for blacks to remain in the South and harvest cotton and other crops that could be sold to northern factories inexpensively. Racism prevented many blacks from getting good educations or jobs in the North.

Whether or not a secret deal had been struck, when Hayes was elected it was clear that the Reconstruction Era was ending. A month after his inauguration, in April 1877, federal troops were withdrawn from South Carolina and Louisiana, the last two states where they were garrisoned.

Removing the federal troops from the South allowed white Democrats to take control in those states. Although the **Redeemers**, as southern Democratic governments after reconstruction became known, could never bring slavery back, they could ensure that whites kept the dominant place in southern society by **disenfranchising** blacks. In all sorts of ways, they made it harder for blacks in the South to prosper. Black Americans were held down both politically and economically, in order to keep them beholden to whites in the southern states.

UNFINISHED WORK

The election of President Hayes and the subsequent withdrawal of troops marked the unofficial end to an incomplete process. Reconstruction had been difficult and violent, and unfortunately it was never really completed. Although black Americans had been granted civil rights by the Thirteenth, Fourteenth, and Fifteenth amendments to the US Constitution, many freedmen wondered whether they would be allowed to exercise their rights.

In 1877, the country was as divided on racial issues as it had ever been. Tensions between blacks and whites were high, and blacks were subject to unfair treatment. It was a difficult and confusing time.

The end of reconstruction marked the beginning of a new period of legal segregation. This was another way for whites to keep blacks from becoming successful in life.

SEGREGATION AND JIM CROW

The term *Jim Crow* is often used to describe the oppressive way of life forced upon black Americans after reconstruction ended. From the late 1870s until the 1960s, Jim Crow laws in the southern

After the Civil War, many freedmen rented land from white plantation owners and raised crops to sell. These farmers, or sharecroppers, paid their rent with a portion of the crop. The sharecropper system meant that blacks did not have to work under the direct supervision of whites on labor contracts. However, if the crops failed the black farmer could wind up in debt to the white landowner. These black workers are taking a break from picking cotton to play a game of dice.

ORIGIN OF THE TERM "JIM CROW"

During the nineteenth century, minstrel shows were a popular form of entertainment. These shows featured songs, dances, and jokes—some of which were borrowed from African-American traditions. The first minstrel shows didn't involve black American performers, however. Instead, white actors portrayed African Americans by wearing makeup called blackface. Minstrel show comedians dressed in baggy clothes, spoke with a strange accent, and acted foolish. White audiences in both the North and the South thought they were funny and enjoyed the songs and dances.

"Jim Crow" was the name of a minstrel show character portrayed by a white actor named Thomas Dartmouth Rice. He was very popular among American audiences during the 1830s and 1840s. Rice would wear old rags for clothing and use burnt coal to make his face black. Then he pretended to be a lazy and unintelligent black man.

Minstrel show characters like Jim Crow helped to perpetuate the stereotype that blacks were inferior to whites. Like many other unacceptable terms, "Jim Crow" was considered a racial slur. While the term was not as ugly as some of the others that were used, it was used to differentiate blacks from whites and to indicate that they were less intelligent and polished than whites.

After Reconstruction, the state laws in the South that imposed segregation and restricted the rights of black people were known as "Jim Crow laws." The use of this mocking term was a clear indication of how most southern whites really felt, and how little respect they had for black Americans.

states took away many legal rights of African Americans. The laws prevented blacks from voting, testifying in court against whites, holding public office, or serving on juries.

Jim Crow laws also prevented whites and blacks from coming in contact with one another in public facilities. "Whites Only" and "Colored Only" signs hung over separate door entrances and exits. There were separate public restrooms, hospitals, schools, and churches. In trains, black passengers had to ride in separate cars from whites.

Preventing black Americans from using the same trains, hotels, and other public facilities as whites seemed like a clear violation of the Civil Rights Act of 1875. But in 1883, the US Supreme Court struck down this Civil Rights Act. The justices declared that Congress didn't have the authority under the Fourteenth Amendment to grant black Americans equal protection under the laws. Only state and local governments, the Supreme Court said, could do that.

Meanwhile, southern states were also finding ways to get around the Fifteenth Amendment. That amendment made it unlawful to deny a person the right to vote based on race or previous status as a slave. But poll taxes prevented many black people from voting. Poor African Americans couldn't afford these special taxes, which had to be paid before a person was eligible to vote. Southern states also imposed literacy tests as a requirement for voting. Many former slaves didn't know how to read and write, because they had no formal education. So literacy tests effectively blocked them from voting.

Of course, many poor whites couldn't afford to pay a poll tax and couldn't read or write either. Seven southern states would eventually solve this problem with a "grandfather clause." This exempted any person from having to pay the poll tax or pass a literacy test if he had an ancestor who'd been eligible to vote before 1867. No blacks fell into that category—but almost all whites did.

A school for black students in Kentucky during the 1890s. Although facilities for blacks and whites were kept separate, they were rarely equal.

A LANDMARK DECISION

In the late nineteenth century, some people decided to challenge racial segregation in the South. One group, made up of both black and white activists, called itself the Citizens' Committee to Test the Constitutionality of the Separate Car Act. It was formed in Louisiana, where a law passed in 1890 required railroads to have separate train cars for white and black passengers.

On June 7, 1892, a thirty-year-old shoemaker and member of the Citizens' Committee boarded an East Louisiana Railroad train in New Orleans and took a seat in the whites-only car. Homer Plessy looked white. Seven of his eight great-grandparents were white. But under the Louisiana law of the time, a single drop of "black" blood made a person black. Plessy informed the conductor about his African-American ancestry, then refused to leave the whites-only car. He was arrested.

In court, Plessy's lawyer argued that his client's civil rights, which were guaranteed under the Fourteenth Amendment, had been violated. The trial judge, John H. Ferguson, rejected this argument. Ferguson found Plessy guilty of violating the Separate Car Act and ordered him to pay a $25 fine.

Plessy appealed the decision. But the Louisiana State Supreme Court sided with Ferguson. After another appeal, the case landed before the US Supreme Court.

On May 18, 1896, the Supreme Court delivered its decision in the case known as *Plessy v. Ferguson*. By a 7–1 majority, the Court found that Louisiana's Separate Car Act didn't violate the Constitution. The justices admitted that the purpose of the Fourteenth Amendment "was undoubtedly to enforce the absolute equality of the two races before the law." But, in the Court's opinion, the amendment

> could not have been intended to abolish distinctions based upon color, or to enforce social, as distinguished from political, equality, or a commingling of the two races upon terms unsatisfactory to either. Laws permitting, and even requiring, their separation, in places where they are liable to be brought into contact, do not necessarily imply the inferiority of either race to the other.

In other words, the Fourteenth Amendment's requirement of equality before the law didn't mean that African Americans were entitled to use the same public facilities as whites. It only meant that blacks had to be provided with public facilities that were similar to the ones whites used. "Separate but equal" treatment of the races, the Court said, was perfectly legal.

With the *Plessy v. Ferguson* decision, Jim Crow had the legal blessing of the Supreme Court. Throughout the South, and sometimes even in other states, more laws were passed to enforce racial segregation. But the idea that the separate accommodations provided to blacks were equal to those enjoyed by whites was fiction. Generally, the facilities for blacks were far below the standards enjoyed by whites. Schools for black children were often not clean or well built, and the books and teaching materials were often not good quality. The "separate but equal" standard of *Plessy v. Ferguson* was a way to make it sound as though blacks were being treated fairly, but it was easy to see that they were not.

Jim Crow ensured that African Americans remained second-class citizens. Conditions for black Americans were worst in the South. But racial segregation existed in other parts of the country as well. And for many decades the federal government did nothing to address the injustices.

Despite the unfair restrictions, blacks tried to build lives they could enjoy and be proud of. They were able to own property and receive an education. However, many struggled with the knowledge that most white people would never accept them as equals. Blacks had to be careful who they looked at, how they spoke to others, and where they traveled. Failure to comply with the unspoken codes of behavior in many communities increased their chances of being harassed, threatened, arrested, or worse.

THE CIVIL RIGHTS MOVEMENT

Finally, in the middle of the twentieth century, some brave African Americans began chipping away at the foundations of Jim Crow. The Civil Rights Movement was a wide-ranging struggle for equality under the law. It was waged by tens of thousands of black Americans. A few would become famous leaders, such as Martin Luther King Jr. Most, however, were ordinary men, women, and young people who had the courage to stand up against injustice. White people, too, joined the Civil Rights Movement.

Civil rights activists used a variety of tactics. They challenged Jim Crow laws in state and federal courts. They held marches and demonstrations. They engaged in acts of civil disobedience, refusing to obey unfair laws and regulations. They organized drives to register African-American voters, especially in southern states.

The body of a black man named George Meadows hangs from a tree in Birmingham, Alabama, in 1889. More than 3,000 blacks were lynched between 1882 and 1919. There was no trial, and often the only crime was that the person was black and outspoken, or simply in the wrong place at the wrong time.

The path toward equality was difficult. Every time African Americans took a step forward, whites who wanted to maintain racial segregation pushed back. There was a resurgence of hate groups, including the Ku Klux Klan, that tried to intimidate blacks into giving up the fight for their rights. Civil rights activists were attacked and beaten. Some lost their lives.

But between the mid-1950s and the mid-1960s, the legal structure of Jim Crow was dismantled. In 1954 the US Supreme Court overturned the *Plessy v. Ferguson* decision, ruling in *Brown v. Board of Education* that segregated schools violated the Fourteenth Amendment to the Constitution. New laws enacted by the federal government banned racial segregation and removed obstacles that prevented black Americans from exercising the right to vote. At last, after centuries of slavery and Jim Crow segregation, all of the nation's black people were promised equality under the law.

This restaurant in Durham, North Carolina, has separate entrances for black and white customers. The photo was taken in the early 1940s.

1. What states' electoral votes were disputed in the 1876 presidential election?

2. Who created the Jim Crow minstrel show character?

3. How did poll taxes and literacy tests prevent blacks from voting?

RESEARCH PROJECT

Using the internet or your school library, learn more about the Compromise of 1877. Write a two-page paper about whether or not history would have been different if federal troops had remained in the South, citing sources to justify your arguments.

antebellum period—refers to the period from 1789, after the United States became an independent nation, until the Civil War began in 1861.

aristocracy—the highest class in a society.

cash crop—a crop, such as cotton or tobacco, that is produced primarily for sale at a market. Cultivation of cash crops was very labor-intensive, and required large numbers of slaves.

chattel slavery—a type of slavery in which the enslaved person becomes the personal property (chattel) of the owner and can be bought, sold, or inherited. The person is a slave for life, and their offspring are also enslaved.

domestic slave trade—the buying, selling, and transportation of enslaved people within a territory or country, such as the United States or the Spanish colonies.

Emancipation Proclamation—a presidential proclamation issued in late 1862 that declared that all African-Americans held as slaves in rebellious states during the Civil War would be considered free by the United States government on January 1, 1863.

indentured servants—a form of servitude in which a person agrees to work in exchange for food and shelter for a certain period of time.

Middle Passage—name for the slave trade route from Africa to America across the Atlantic Ocean, which was infamous due to its horrific conditions.

overseer—a plantation manager who supervised the work activities of slaves.

Quaker—a member of the Religious Society of Friends, a Christian group that was strongly opposed to slavery.

segregation—the separation of people in their daily lives based on race.

sharecropper—a tenant farmer in the South who was given credit by the landowner to pay for seeds, tools, living quarters, and food, in exchange for a share of his crop at the time of harvesting.

tenant farmer—a person who farms on rented land.

transatlantic slave trade—the capturing, enslaving, buying, selling, and transportation of Africans across the Atlantic to the Americas.

Underground Railroad—term for the route used by runaway slaves to reach freedom, either in the Northern states or Canada.

white supremacy—a belief that white people are superior to people of all other races, especially the black race, and should therefore dominate society.

slave codes—laws passed in the South to restrict the activity of slaves. Some laws made it illegal to teach slaves how to read or write. Others prevented slaves from moving freely from place to place without a pass, or from holding religious services without the presence of a white man to monitor their activities.

CHRONOLOGY

1865 The Civil War ends and Lincoln is assassinated in April. Andrew Johnson becomes president and implements a reconstruction plan. The Thirteenth Amendment is ratified in June. In Mississippi, the first Black Codes are enacted; other states soon follow.

1866 Republicans in Congress override Johnson's vetoes to passes important legislation, including the Civil Rights Act and an expansion of the mission of the Freedmen's Bureau. Race riots occur in New Orleans, Louisiana, and Memphis, Tennessee.

1867 Congress passes three Reconstruction Acts over the president's veto. At the Republican Convention in New Orleans, the party proposes a platform supporting equality for black Americans.

1868 The fourth Reconstruction Act is passed. Oscar J. Dunn, a former slave, is elected as lieutenant governor in Louisiana. John W. Menard is elected to represent Louisiana in the House of Representatives, but is not permitted to take his seat. In July, the Fourteenth Amendment is ratified.

1869 Ulysses S. Grant is inaugurated as president in March. Grant is an ally of Congress' Radical Republicans, but not a strong supporter of Reconstruction.

1870 The Fifteenth Amendment to the U.S. Constitution, ratified on February 3, prohibits states and the federal government from using a citizen's race, color, or previous status as a slave as a voting qualification. Hiram Revels of Mississippi becomes the first black man elected to the US Senate. The first Enforcement Act is passed to protect the civil rights of black Americans in the South.

1871 Congress passes a second Enforcement Act and the Ku Klux Klan Act. Five blacks are elected to serve in the House of Representatives.

1872   The Freedmen's Bureau is abolished. The growing unpopularity of reconstruction leads some dissatisfied Republicans to challenge the incumbent president, but Grant wins re-election.

1873   P.B.S. Pinchback serves as acting governor of Louisiana, becoming the first black man to serve as a state governor. His tenure ends after a few months due to white resistance. About 150 blacks are massacred by white Democrats at Colfax, Louisiana.

1874   Blanche K Bruce and Robert Smalls and elected to the US Senate and the US Congress, respectively.

1875   The Civil Rights Act is enacted by Congress, but later declared unconstitutional by the Supreme Court. Mississippi elects a black Senator, who becomes the first to complete the entirety of a six-year term.

1876   The US Senate votes against seating P.B.S. Pinchback. Wade Hampton, who was a leader in the Confederacy, becomes governor of South Carolina.

1877   Rutherford B. Hayes is elected president of the United States in a disputed election. A few weeks after his inauguration, Hayes withdraws federal troops from South Carolina, ending the Reconstruction Era.

1896   The Supreme Court's *Plessy v. Ferguson* decision upholds segregation laws, so long as the standard of "separate but equal" is met.

1964   Congress passes a new Civil Rights Act, which prohibits racial discrimination in the United States. It is followed the next year by the Voting Rights Act, which enforces the protections given to black Americans by the Fourteenth and Fifteenth Amendments.

FURTHER READING

Du Bois, W.E.B. *Black Reconstruction in America: An Essay toward a History of the Part which Black Folk Played in the Attempt to Reconstruct Democracy in America, 1860-1880*. Edited by Henry Louis Gates. New York, Oxford University Press, 2007.

Foner, Eric. *Reconstruction: America's Unfinished Revolution, 1863-1877*. New York: Harper Perennial Modern Classics, 2014.

Gienapp, William E., ed. *The Civil War and Reconstruction: A Documentary Collection*. New York: W.W. Norton & Co., 2001.

Guelzo, Allen C. *Reconstruction: A Concise History*. New York, Oxford University Press, 2018.

Perman, Michael, ed. *Major Problems in the Civil War and Reconstruction*. New York: Wadsworth, 2010.

Prince, K. Stephen. *Radical Reconstruction: A Brief History with Documents*. New York: Bedford/St. Martin's, 2015.

Simpson, Brooks D. *Reconstruction: Voices from America's First Great Struggle for Racial Equality*. New York: The Library of America, 2018.

INTERNET RESOURCES

www.history.com/topics/american-civil-war/reconstruction

The History Channel's online synopsis provides a timeline of reconstruction in text format, along with video explaining what America went through during that time period.

www.howard.edu/library/reference/guides/reconstructionera

The Howard University library system offers a concise and comprehensive synopsis of reconstruction, and provides links that can be followed for further information.

www.britannica.com/event/Reconstruction-United-States-history

Encyclopaedia Brittanica offers a longer synopsis of the Reconstruction Era and how it eventually ended, with sources, links to further reading, and a large amount of related information to explore.

www.digitalhistory.uh.edu/exhibits/reconstruction/introduction.html

Digital History breaks down the reconstruction period into sections, allowing exploration of just one particular area of that time period, and provides links for further reading and resources, as well.

www.nytimes.com/2015/03/29/opinion/sunday/why-reconstruction-matters.html

This *New York Times* piece is an opinion, but it is a powerful way to learn more about how history is viewed by others, not just the facts that took place during that time.

https://www.facinghistory.org/reconstruction-era/video-series

Facing History and Ourselves is a charitable organization that has created a seven-video series used to teach about reconstruction. It provides new insights into the events that took place in American history during that time.

p. 12   "The rebels are numerous and powerful..." Charles Sumner, "Union and Peace! How They Shall Be Restored," speech before the Republican state convention, at Worcester, Mass. (October 1, 1861). Available at https://archive.org/details/unionandpeacehow00sumnrich/page/2

p. 20   "with malice toward none..." Abraham Lincoln, "Second Inaugural Address," (March 4, 1865). Available at https://www.ourdocuments.gov/doc.php?flash=false&doc=38

p. 24   "we all agree..." Abraham Lincoln, "Last Public Address," (April 11, 1865). Available at http://www.abrahamlincolnonline.org/lincoln/speeches/last.htm

p. 25   "the re-inauguration of the national authority..." Lincoln, "Last Public Address."

p. 25   "Let 'em up easy." Abraham Lincoln, quoted in Kevin Morrow, "Lincoln's Triumphant Visit to Richmond," New York Times (April 7, 2015). https://opinionator.blogs.nytimes.com/2015/04/07/lincolns-triumphant-visit-to-richmond/

p. 39   "all civil and political rights ..." Report of the Joint Committee on Reconstruction (Washington, D.C.: Government Printing Office, 1866). https://archive.org/details/journalofjointco03unit/page/28

p. 46   "I tell you that the Negro ..." Joseph Rainey, quoted in Congressional Record, House, 43rd Cong., 1st sess. (December 19, 1873), p. 344.

p. 51   "The violence in the South ..." Clarence Walker, quoted in "Southern Violence During Reconstruction," PBS American Experience (accessed March 2019). https://www.pbs.org/wgbh/americanexperience/features/reconstruction-southern-violence-during-reconstruction/

p. 65   "was undoubtedly to enforce . . ." *Plessy v. Ferguson*, 163 U.S. 537 (1896). http://caselaw.lp.findlaw.com/scripts/getcase.pl?court=us&vol=163&invol=537

p. 65   "could not have been intended . . ." Ibid.

INDEX

INDEX

AUTHOR'S BIOGRAPHY

Michelle Dakota Beck has worked as a freelance writer since 1994. During that time she has produced both fiction and nonfiction books, ebooks, articles, web pages, product descriptions, white papers, and much more for clients all over the world. In her spare time she enjoys reading, exercise, train travel, and playing violin and piano. Michelle lives in Washington State.

CREDITS